THE WORLD OF
OLYMPICS

Nick Hunter

Heinemann
LIBRARY

Chicago, Illinois

www.heinemannraintree.com
Visit our website to find out
more information about
Heinemann-Raintree books.

To order:

☎ Phone 888-454-2279

💻 Visit www.heinemannraintree.com
to browse our catalog and order online.

Edited by Kate de Villiers and Laura Knowles
Designed by Richard Parker
Picture research by Liz Alexander
Production by Camilla Crask
Originated by Capstone Global Library Ltd
Printed and bound in China by CTPS

15 14 13 12
10 9 8 7 6 5 4 3

Library of Congress Cataloging-in-Publication Data
Hunter, Nick.
  The world of Olympics / Nick Hunter.
    p. cm.—(The Olympics)
  Includes bibliographical references and index.
  ISBN 978-1-4109-4120-6 (hc)—ISBN 978-1-4109-4126-8 (pb)
  1. Olympics—History. I. Title.
  GV721.5.H85 2012
  796.48—dc22   2010049493

Acknowledgments
We would like to thank the following for permission to
reproduce photographs: Alamy pp. **5** (© Aflo Foto Agency),
6 (© ACE STOCK LIMITED), **7** (© INTERFOTO), **20**
(© The Print Collector); Corbis pp. **9** (© Gero Breloer /epa),
15 (© Clifford White), **16** (© Reuters/Dylan Martinez), **17**
(© Thierry Orban/Sygma), **19** (© Paul Chinn/San Francisco
Chronicle), **21** (© Peter Foley/epa), **23** (© Alexandros Vlachos/
epa), **24** (© Stephen Hird/Reuters); Dreamstime.com p. **10**
(© Georgios Alexandris); Getty Images pp. **8** (Hulton Archive),
18 (Mike Powell /Allsport), **27** (Bob Thomas); Photolibrary
pp. **11** (Andrew Paterson), **22** (EPA/Kim Ludbrook),
Shutterstock pp. **13** (© mary416).

Cover photograph of the opening ceremony of the 1988 Winter
Olympics in Calgary, Canada, reproduced with permission of
Corbis/© Gilbert Iundt; Jean-Yves Ruszniewski/TempSport.

Every effort has been made to contact copyright holders of
material reproduced in this book. Any omissions will be
rectified in subsequent printings if notice is given to the
publisher.

Contents

Some words are shown in bold, **like this**. You can find them in the glossary on page 30.

The World's Games

The opening ceremony was nearly over. As people held their breath in the **stadium**, a lone athlete seemed to float around the rim of the stadium. He then lit the Olympic flame with his burning **torch**. The Olympic Games had begun!

Festival of sports

The Summer Olympic Games is the world's greatest sporting event. Every four years, athletes from more than 200 nations compete in around 300 different sporting events. The Winter Olympic Games are also held every four years for winter sports, such as skiing and snowboarding. The athletes want to be the best in their sport and take home the winner's gold medal.

Some countries, such as China and the United States, send hundreds of athletes. They expect to win many medals. Other countries may only send a few athletes and are happy to win one medal. Afghanistan won its first medal at the 2008 Olympics in Beijing, China.

Olympic controversy

Although the Olympics are about bringing people together, the Games have had their fair share of arguments and crises. Disagreements between countries have meant some athletes have not been allowed to compete at the Olympics. Some athletes have cheated by taking **drugs** to win medals.

The 2008 Beijing Olympic Games began with a spectacular opening ceremony.

The Olympic Creed

"The most important thing in life is not the triumph, but the fight; the essential thing is not to have won, but to have fought well"

How It All Began

The first Olympic Games were held nearly 2,800 years ago, in 776 BCE. Every four years, athletes from around **ancient Greece** would meet at Olympia. The first Olympics only included one sporting event—the *stade*, or sprint race. Over the years more events were added, such as boxing and discus throwing.

The modern Olympics

In 1890, Baron Pierre de Coubertin had the idea of bringing back the Olympic Games. The first modern Games were held in Athens, Greece, in 1896.

Pankration was the most violent sport at the ancient Olympics. This cross between boxing and wrestling is not part of the modern Games.

Olympic fact file: Athens 1896

Countries: 14
Athletes: 245 men, 0 women
Most successful country: United States

- Spiridon Louis of Greece won the first official **marathon** race, from Marathon to Athens.
- Swimming events were held in the cold sea. One athlete said, "my will to live … overcame my desire to win!"

Spiridon Louis of Greece won the marathon at the 1896 Athens Olympics. The runner who finished third was **disqualified** for taking a lift from a carriage for part of the route.

PIERRE DE COUBERTIN (1863-1937)

Coubertin was a French **nobleman**. His belief that sports were important for health was unusual at the time. He organized the first modern Games and led the **Olympic Movement** for many years.

Every Nation on Earth

Athletes from almost every country compete at today's Olympics. But the first modern Olympics only included athletes from 14 nations, who had done very little training. In 1896 Irishman John Boland was in Greece visiting a friend and joined in the tennis competition. He won two gold medals.

Every four years, the Games are held in a different city. Paris in 1900 was the first Olympics where women competed. Today just under half of all athletes at the Summer Olympics are women.

Britain's Charlotte Cooper was the first Olympic women's champion when she won the tennis singles in Paris. Athletes' clothing has changed a lot since 1900!

The Games get going

The modern Olympics became more popular after the first London Olympics in 1908. The first Winter Olympics were held in 1924. Despite breaks for the two World Wars (1914–1918 and 1939–1945), the Olympics were here to stay. The London 2012 Olympic Games are the 27th modern Games, and the third in London.

At the start of the Games, one athlete takes the Olympic oath, on behalf of all the athletes, promising to abide by the rules and compete "in the spirit of **sportsmanship**."

Medal tables

Individuals and teams, rather than countries, win medals at the Olympics. However, there is strong competition to be the top country and lead the medal table. The United States has topped the medal table more times than any other nation.

Symbols of the Olympics

There are three main **symbols** that can be seen at every Olympics. They each **symbolize** a different value.

The Olympic flame

The lighting of the Olympic flame in the **stadium** is the key moment of the opening ceremony. The flame stays lit until the closing ceremony. Several months before the Games, the flame is lit by the Sun's rays at Olympia in Greece. It is then taken to the host city by a relay of runners carrying burning **torches**. The Olympic flame symbolizes friendship.

The Olympic motto

The Olympic **motto** is "*Citius, Altius, Fortius,*" which means "Faster, Higher, Stronger" in Latin. The motto symbolizes excellence.

The Olympic torch relay travels through many countries before arriving in the host city.

The Olympic flag

The rings on the Olympic flag represent the five continents competing. Every country's flag includes one of the colors of the Olympic rings. The flag symbolizes respect for every nation.

The Olympic flag is raised during the Games.

The Olympic Movement

The **International Olympic Committee (IOC)** is in charge of the Olympic Games. It is based in Lausanne, Switzerland. The IOC's members have the important job of deciding where the Games will be held. The IOC works with National Olympic Committees from each country and the people in charge of each sport to stage the Olympics. Together they make up the **Olympic Movement**.

The Olympics in Asia

In 2008, the Olympics were held in Beijing, China. These Games were probably the most spectacular ever seen, as well as the most expensive ever held, costing more than $40 billion.

Chinese gold rush

China topped the medal table in Beijing for the first time, with 51 gold medals. Chinese athletes dominated sports such as gymnastics, diving, and weightlifting. However, China's great track star Liu Xiang, who won the men's 110-meter hurdles at the Athens Olympics in 2004, was injured and could not take part.

Other Asian nations also have strong Olympic records. South Korea won more gold medals in Beijing than ever before. India's men's hockey team went through six Olympics without defeat until they were beaten in the 1960 final by their bitter rivals, Pakistan.

Olympic fact file: Beijing 2008

Countries: 204

Athletes: 6,305 men, 4,637 women

Most successful country: China

- More than 40 world records were broken.
- U.S. swimmer Michael Phelps won eight gold medals to go with the six he had won in Athens in 2004—the most gold medals ever won by an athlete at a single Games, and the most in total.

The stunning "Bird's Nest" **stadium** in Beijing was built specially for the Games. The dramatic opening ceremony was held here.

Other Asian Olympics

Before Beijing, Asia had held the Summer Olympic Games twice:

- Seoul, South Korea (1988)
- Tokyo, Japan (1964)

Japan has also held the Winter Olympics twice: first in Sapporo (1972) and then in Nagano (1998).

Games Down Under

For many people, the Sydney Olympic Games of 2000 were the best ever. The highlight for many Australians was the **Aboriginal**-Australian Cathy Freeman winning the 400 meters. For others, the star was British rower Steve Redgrave, who became the first athlete to win gold medals at five Olympics in a row.

Australia also hosted the 1956 Olympics in Melbourne. The horse-riding events took place in Stockholm, Sweden, because of Australia's strict rules about bringing animals into the country. This is the only time the Games have been held in two countries.

Slow boat to the Olympics

Australia has competed in the Olympics since 1896. Athletes made long journeys by sea to get to European Olympics. It took the New Zealand team nine weeks to get to Antwerp for their first Olympics as a separate team in 1920.

Olympic fact file: Sydney 2000

Countries: 200

Athletes: 6,580 men, 4,069 women

Most successful country: United States

- **Triathlon**, tae kwon do, and synchronized diving were Olympic events for the first time.
- The Bahamas became the smallest country to win a team event when their women's team won the 4 x 100-meter relay.

Australia's greatest Olympians

Ian Thorpe (below) is one of Australia's greatest swimmers. He won five gold medals between 2000 and 2004. Other great Australian Olympians were Betty Cuthbert, who won three athletics gold medals in 1956, and Dawn Fraser, who won swimming golds at three different Olympics.

Out of Africa

The Olympics have never been held in Africa, but African athletes have made their mark on the Games. Since Abebe Bikila won the **marathon** with bare feet in 1960, Ethiopians and Kenyans have dominated distance running.

Why do these countries produce so many great runners? There are a number of reasons, including tough training methods and the effects of living and running in the mountains. Many of these athletes come from poor communities. Running requires almost no equipment. It can be a way for these amazing athletes to earn money and respect.

African teams have won medals in Olympic soccer. Nigeria won gold in 1996 and silver in 2008. Cameroon (above) won gold in 2000.

Ethiopian sprinter Haile Gebrselassie is one of the greatest athletes of all time.

Five great African runners

- Abebe Bikila (Ethiopia): won the marathon in 1960 and 1964. He ran barefoot when he won gold in 1960.
- Maria Mutola (Mozambique): Mutola ran the 800 meters at the Olympics six times, winning one gold and one bronze medal.
- Haile Gebrselassie (Ethiopia): as a child, Gebrselassie ran 10 kilometers to school every day. As an adult, he won the Olympic 10,000 meters twice.
- Tirunesh Dibaba (Ethiopia): women's Olympic champion at 5,000 and 10,000 meters in 2008.
- Kenenisa Bekele (Ethiopia): three Olympic titles at 5,000 and 10,000 meters.

Olympic North America

The United States has been the most successful Olympic nation since the first modern Olympics in 1896. The United States has two of the most successful Olympic athletes of all time. Michael Phelps has won an astonishing 14 gold medals. Carl Lewis won nine gold medals in sprinting and long jump in the 1980s. U.S. athletes have also dominated team sports. The U.S. women's basketball team won four gold medals in a row from 1996 to 2008.

Michael Johnson is one of America's greatest athletes ever. His victories in the 200 and 400 meters made him a star at the 1996 Atlanta Games.

St. Louis 1904

The Olympics were first held in North America in 1904. The St. Louis Games were not a success. Only 12 countries sent athletes, and half the events included only Americans. Two African athletes were the first Africans to compete at the Olympics.

The Summer Olympics have been held four times in the United States, and once in Canada and Mexico. North America has held the Winter Olympics six times, including Vancouver, Canada, in 2010.

In the exciting sport of ski cross, athletes race against each other over jumps and around tight corners on an uneven course.

Olympic fact file: Vancouver Winter Olympics 2010

Countries: 82

Athletes: 1,503 men, 1,033 women

Most successful country: Canada

- Canada's 14 gold medals were the most won by any country at the Winter Olympics.
- Ski cross was included in the Winter Olympics for the first time.

Controversy at the Olympics

With so many countries involved, it is no surprise that politics have sometimes intruded into the Olympic Games.

Hitler's Olympics

The 1936 Olympic Games were held in Berlin, the capital of Nazi Germany. The Nazis and their leader, Adolf Hitler, believed that they were better than other races of people. African-American athlete Jesse Owens was not put off by Hitler's **racist** ideas. He won four gold medals, including one for the 100 meters.

Jesse Owens's success at the 1936 Olympics was a fitting response to Hitler's racist beliefs.

Tragedy and boycotts

At the 1972 Munich Olympics, eleven Israeli athletes were murdered by Palestinian **terrorists**. Many countries, including the United States, **boycotted** the 1980 Moscow Olympics for political reasons. Athletes from the **Soviet Union** and its allies then boycotted the Los Angeles Games in 1984. Tiny Albania boycotted four Olympic Games in a row for different reasons between 1976 and 1988.

Marion Jones of the United States finished first in the 100 meters in Sydney, but was **disqualified** after admitting to using drugs.

Drugs at the Olympics

Some athletes have tried to cheat at the Olympics by taking **drugs** to improve their performance. This is against the rules. Drugs affect many sports, but have been an especially big issue in athletics. Two Olympic 100-meter gold medallists have had their medals taken away after admitting to drug use.

From Athens to Athens—the Olympics in Europe

From Athens in 1896 to London in 2012, more than half of the Summer Olympic Games have been held in Europe. In 2004, the Games returned to Athens, where they had started in 1896.

European Olympics have seen great sporting achievements. Dutch athlete Fanny Blankers-Koen won four gold medals in London in 1948. Czech runner Emil Zatopek earned an amazing three golds, winning the 5,000 meters, 10,000 meters, and the **marathon** at the Helsinki Games in 1952. His wife, the athlete Dana Zatopkova, won a gold medal in the javelin, too.

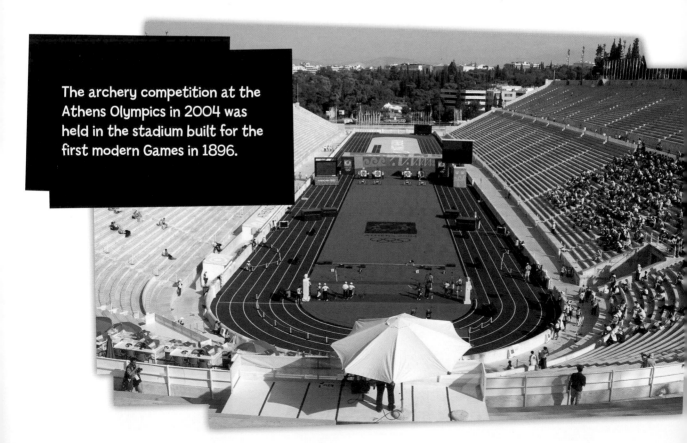

The archery competition at the Athens Olympics in 2004 was held in the stadium built for the first modern Games in 1896.

Paralympics

The **Paralympic Games** grew from a sporting event held in the
United Kingdom at the same time as the second London Olympics in
1948. The event was for soldiers injured in World War II. The first
official Paralympics for disabled athletes were held in Rome in 1960.

Russia's Natalia
Goudkova throws the
javelin to win silver
at the Athens 2004
Paralympic Games.

Olympic fact file: Athens 2004

Countries: 201
Athletes: 6,255 men, 4,305 women
Most successful country: United States

- The shot put competition was held in the **stadium** at
  Olympia, the home of the ancient Olympic Games.
- The United Kingdom's Kelly Holmes won the
  women's 800 and 1,500 meters.
- Morocco's Hicham El Guerrouj won the men's 1,500
  and 5,000 meters.

The World Comes to London

As the Beijing Olympics closed in 2008, athletes were invited to meet again in London in the United Kingdom in four years time.

At that time, a huge Olympic Park was already being built on old industrial land in east London. The park would include a new Olympic **Stadium**, an Aquatics Center for swimming and diving, and many other sporting venues. Other sports would be held in famous arenas such as Wimbledon tennis club and Wembley Stadium.

London's Olympic Games in 2012 hopes to inspire many young people to take up sports.

Olympic headaches

London has faced many of the same problems as previous Olympic cities. Organizing an event for 10,000 athletes and many more spectators takes years and costs billions of dollars. In addition to this, London and the Olympic Games have both been targets for **terrorist** attacks in the past, so **security** is very important. This takes careful planning and organization.

Olympic triple

London is the first city to host the Olympic Games three times. In 1908 London was the first city to build a new Olympic stadium. The city also hosted the first Games after World War II, in 1948. It was only three years after the end of the war, and London was still recovering from the heavy bombing of the war years. These were also the first Olympic Games to be shown on home television, although very few people owned a television set at the time.

Where Next?

In 2016 the Olympic Games will go to South America for the first time. Rio de Janeiro, on the coast of Brazil, is one of the world's most beautiful cities.

The Brazilians' love of sports is well known. Their amazing soccer team has won the World Cup a record five times. Amazingly, Brazil has never won a soccer gold medal at the Olympics. Brazil's great South American rival, Argentina, won the men's soccer gold in Athens and Beijing. At recent Games, Brazil's athletes have starred in the volleyball and beach volleyball events.

Looking to the future

The Olympic Games can bring great change to a city. New sports arenas and transportation links have to be built. Rio de Janeiro has many problems, including huge numbers of people living in extreme poverty. The excitement and goodwill that the Olympics bring will help this amazing city to build for the future.

Olympic oddities

The Olympics has come a long way. In the early days there was often confusion about which events were even part of the Olympics. Some of the more unusual events included:

- 100-meter freestyle swimming for members of the Greek navy (Athens, 1896)
- ballooning and obstacle-race swimming (Paris, 1900)
- pole-climbing (St. Louis, 1904)

The 2016 Olympics in Rio will bring the world's greatest sporting event to sport-crazy Brazilians for the first time.

A World of Olympics

The world map on page 29 shows every city that has hosted the modern Summer or Winter Olympic Games, and also includes the cities that have been picked to host future Olympic Games.

Summer Olympics medals table

Norway has won the most medals at the Winter Olympics. Look at the table below to find out which countries have won the most medals at the Summer Olympic Games.

Country	Gold	Silver	Bronze
USA	943	736	642
Soviet Union (competed between 1924 and 1988)	395	319	296
United Kingdom	216	272	257
France	211	225	258
Italy	203	168	178
Germany (excludes separate East and West German teams between 1968 and 1988)	202	229	253
Hungary	162	148	163
East Germany (competed between 1968 and 1988)	153	129	127
Sweden	143	165	181
Australia	131	140	168

Hosts of the modern Olympic Games

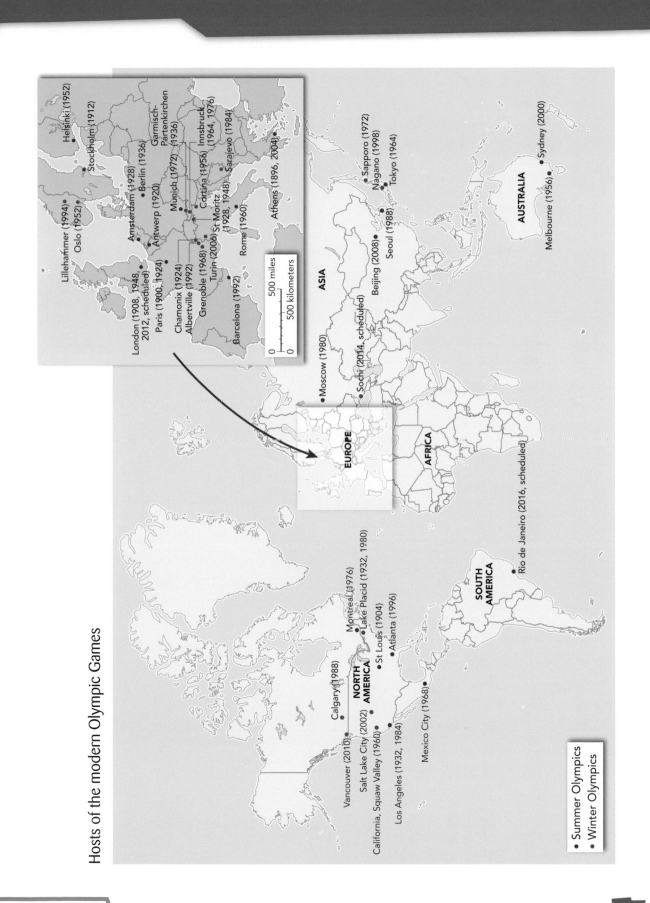

London (1908, 1948, 2012, scheduled)
Paris (1900, 1924)
Lillehammer (1994)
Oslo (1952)
Helsinki (1952)
Stockholm (1912)
Amsterdam (1928)
Antwerp (1920)
Berlin (1936)
Garmisch-Partenkirchen (1936)
Munich (1972)
Chamonix (1924)
Albertville (1992)
Grenoble (1968)
Turin (2006)
St Moritz (1928, 1948)
Cortina (1956)
Innsbruck (1964, 1976)
Sarajevo (1984)
Rome (1960)
Barcelona (1992)
Athens (1896, 2004)

500 miles
500 kilometers

Moscow (1980)
Sochi (2014, scheduled)
Beijing (2008)
Seoul (1988)
Sapporo (1972)
Nagano (1998)
Tokyo (1964)
Sydney (2000)
Melbourne (1956)

ASIA
AUSTRALIA
EUROPE
AFRICA
SOUTH AMERICA
NORTH AMERICA

Calgary (1988)
Vancouver (2010)
Salt Lake City (2002)
California, Squaw Valley (1960)
Los Angeles (1932, 1984)
Mexico City (1968)
Montreal (1976)
Lake Placid (1932, 1980)
St Louis (1904)
Atlanta (1996)
Rio de Janeiro (2016, scheduled)

• Summer Olympics
• Winter Olympics

Glossary

Aboriginal original people of Australia. Aboriginal people lived in Australia for more than 45,000 years before settlers arrived from Europe.

ancient Greece several different city-states, including Athens and Sparta, that were in the area that is modern Greece more than 2000 years ago.

boycott stay away from an event, often for political reasons

disqualify stop someone from being part of a race or competition because they have broken the rules

drug substance that affects the way your body or mind works. Using drugs can give some athletes an unfair advantage, but damages their health.

International Olympic Committee (IOC) organization that runs the Olympic Games and decides where they will be held

marathon long running race held over 26 miles and 385 yards (42.2 kilometers)

motto few words that sum up the aims of a group. The Olympic motto is "Faster, Higher, Stronger."

nobleman someone from a wealthy or privileged family

Olympic Movement all the people involved in the Olympic Games, including the International Olympic Committee, Olympic officials from each country, and each Olympic sport

Paralympic Games games for athletes with a disability, held after the Olympic Games in the same place

racist judging people based on where they come from and the color of their skin. Most people believe that racism is wrong and that people should be judged as individuals.

security keeping people safe

Soviet Union state made up of Russia and several neighboring countries. The Soviet Union existed between 1922 and 1991.

sportsmanship behaving fairly and following rules

stadium large arena for sporting events. The Olympic Stadium is used for athletic events and the opening and closing ceremonies.

symbol sign that represents something else. The Olympic flag shows that the Olympic Games are about respect for all nations.

symbolize to mean or be a sign for something else

terrorist person who uses violence against the public for political reasons

torch something held in the hand with a light or flame at one end

triathlon sports contest with three events, usually swimming, running, and cycling

Find Out More

Books

Christopher, Matt. *The Olympics: Legendary Sports Events*. New York: Little, Brown Books for Young Readers, 2008.

Gifford, Clive. *Summer Olympics: The Definitive Guide to the World's Greatest Sports Celebration*. New York: Kingfisher, 2004.

Johnson, Robin. *Paralympic Sports Events*. New York: Crabtree Publishing, 2009.

Macy, Sue. *Freeze Frame: A Photographic History of the Winter Olympics*. Washington, D.C.: National Geographic Children's Books, 2006.

Macy, Sue. *Swifter, Higher, Stronger: A Photographic History of the Summer Olympics*. Washington, D.C.: National Geographic Children's Books, 2008.

Websites

www.london2012.com
The website of the London 2012 Games includes details of venues and preparations for the Games, as well as information about Olympic sports.

www.olympic.org
The official website of the International Olympic Committee includes facts and statistics about every Olympic Games and every medal winner.

www.paralympic.org
This is the official website of the Paralympic movement.

To find out about the different countries competing at the Olympics, you can search for the National Olympic Committee of each country.

Index